Dudley and Mable Lynn:
A LESSON IN FORGIVENESS

COPYRIGHT © 2024

CATRINA FUENTES

All rights are reserved. No part of this book may be reproduced, distributed, or transmitted in any form or by any means, including photocopying, recording, or other electronic or mechanical methods, without the prior written permission of the author, except in the case of brief quotations embodied in critical reviews and certain other noncommercial uses permitted by copyright law.

Winter had arrived in the rolling hills of Dudley and Mable Lynn's pasture. The air was crisp, the ground frosty, and the trees wore shimmering coats of ice that sparkled like diamonds in the morning sun. Despite the cold, Dudley the bull and Mable Lynn the cow found joy in the small things that made winter special.

"Look at those snowflakes, Dudley!" Mable Lynn exclaimed one morning her breath creating little puffs in the cold air. "They're dancing just for us!" Dudley smiled, watching the snow drift down. "They sure are pretty," he agreed, his deep voice warm and gentle. "Almost as pretty as that patch of clover you love so much."

Mable Lynn's eyes
lit up at the mention of clover.
"Oh, yes! That's my favorite
spot in the whole pasture.
The sweetest clover grows there,
especially during winter when everything
else is sleeping under the snow

One chilly afternoon, while Mable Lynn was napping under the oak tree, wrapped in warm sunbeams, Dudley found himself wandering near
her special clover patch.
His stomach rumbled as he noticed the fresh green leaves
peeking through the frost.

Oh, look!" Dudley whispered to himself, his nose twitching at the sweet scent. "Mable Lynn's favorite clover. She won't mind if I just have a little nibble, will she? We share everything else, after all.

But the clover was so deliciously sweet
that one nibble turned into two, then three.
"Just one more taste," he kept telling himself,
until before he knew it, he had
eaten every last leaf in the patch.
When Mable Lynn woke up from her nap,
she stretched and smiled, looking
forward to her afternoon treat.
"Time for my favorite part of the day,"
she said cheerfully, trotting
over to her clover patch.
But when she arrived, her heart
sank like a stone in the pond.

"Where's my clover?" she cried out, her voice trembling with disbelief. "It was right here, all fresh and..." Then she noticed Dudley standing nearby, looking unusually interested in his hooves, his expression guilty as could be.

"Dudley," she said softly,
her voice quivering with hurt,
"did you... did you eat all my clover?"
Dudley couldn't meet her eyes.
He shuffled his hooves in the frost,
his heart heavy with shame.
"I'm so sorry, Mable Lynn,"
he said, his voice barely above a whisper.
"I didn't mean to eat it all. I thought...
I thought there was enough for
both of us, but I got carried away.
The clover was just so sweet, and before
I knew it..."

Mable Lynn's eyes filled with tears that threatened to freeze in the winter air. "That was my favorite clover, Dudley. My special place. You didn't even save me a single bite!" Her voice caught in her throat. "How could you?"

Before Dudley could respond, she turned
and walked away, her head low
and her heart hurting too much to hear his
desperate apologies echoing across the frosty field.
For days, Mable Lynn avoided Dudley, choosing
to graze alone on the far side of the pasture.
She felt hurt and disappointed every time
she passed the empty clover patch

From afar, she could see Dudley trying his best to make things right. "Mable Lynn!" he would call out hopefully. "I found some really juicy grass over here. It's almost as sweet as clover!"

But Mable Lynn would just shake her head and walk away, her heart still heavy. During their usual game time, Dudley would try again. "I'll be the seeker today," he'd offer, his voice gentle. "And I promise to count extra slow, just the way you like it." "No thank you, Dudley," she'd reply softly, turning away to hide the tears in her eyes.

One peaceful afternoon, Mable Lynn lay by the oak tree, staring at the empty patch where her clover used to grow. Snowflakes drifted down softly around her as she thought about all of Dudley's attempts to apologize. "He really has been trying so hard," she murmured to herself. As she watched the snow fall, a gentle voice in her heart whispered, Everyone makes mistakes. Forgiveness can grow, just like clover. Mable Lynn sighed, her breath creating a small cloud in the cold air. "Maybe I was too hard on Dudley," she thought aloud. "He didn't mean to hurt me. He's always been such a good friend.

Just then, something caught her eye –
a tiny spot of green against the white snow.
She looked down and gasped, her eyes
widening with wonder.
"Oh my goodness!" she exclaimed.
Tiny clover sprouts were pushing
through the frost-covered soil,
their brave little leaves reaching for the winter sun.

Mable Lynn's heart leaped with joy. "The clover is growing back! Just like friendship can grow back too!" Without hesitation, she ran through the snowy pasture to find Dudley. She found him sitting alone by the frozen pond, his reflection showing how sad he looked. His ears were drooping, and he was drawing patterns in the snow with his hoof.

"Dudley!" she called out, her voice warm and excited. "Dudley, I have something important to tell you!" Dudley turned quickly, his ears perking up at her friendly tone. "Yes, Mable Lynn?" he asked hopefully, hardly daring to believe she was actually speaking to him again.

"I forgive you," she said, smiling warmly. "I know you didn't mean to eat all the clover. And guess what? The most wonderful thing has happened – it's growing back! Little tiny sprouts, right through the snow!"

Dudley's whole face lit up like the morning sun.
"Really? Oh, Mable Lynn, that's wonderful news!"
he exclaimed, his voice full of joy.
Then he grew serious. "Thank you for forgiving me.
I promise to be more thoughtful next time.
Maybe... maybe we could share the
clover when it grows back?"
"I'd love that," Mable Lynn said, nuzzling her
friend gently.
"After all, everything is better when we share it."

From that day on Dudley and Mable Lynn shared everything the sweet clover patches, the juiciest grass, and all their favorite snow-covered adventures.

During their walks together, they would stop by the clover patch to check on the growing sprouts.

"Look how much they've grown!" Mable Lynn would say excitedly. "Just like our friendship," Dudley would reply with a warm smile.
They learned that forgiveness, like clover, grows best when given time, care, and love.

And as the winter days passed, their friendship grew stronger and deeper, just like the roots of the sweet clover
in their special patch of pasture,
reaching down through the frozen ground to find warmth in the earth.